DEEP ROOTS IN A DRY PLACE

An Illustrated Poetic Natural
History of Sonoran Desert Plants

SALLY BENNETT BOYINGTON

With AI-generated images and
comparison poems by ChatGPT

Wordsmith Pages

© 2024 by Sally Bennett Boyington
Photographs © 1982–2024
All rights reserved.

As of 2023, the U.S. Copyright Office does not recognize copyright protection for content created by humans using generative AI such as Midjourney, DALL-E, Stable Diffusion, and ChatGPT. This may change in the future; for now, however, "sufficiently creative" human arrangements or modifications of AI-generated material such as the design of the pages presenting AI content in this book may be copyrighted. Please respect the intention and efforts of the author and do not reproduce the AI-generated poems and images in this book.

The poems, explanatory text, and photographs by Sally Bennett Boyington are protected by copyright.

ISBN: 978-1-951303-15-0

"Century Plant," awarded first place in the September 2023 Arizona State Poetry Society contest, was originally published in *Sandcutters 2023*, the ASPS anthology volume.

Contents

Preface	v
Introduction	1
Barrel Cactus (*Ferocactus* spp.)	8
Brittlebush (*Encelia farinosa*)	10
Cattail (*Typha domingensis*)	12
Century Plant (*Agave* spp.)	14
Cholla (*Cylindropuntia* spp.)	16
Common Reed (*Phragmites communis*)	18
Creosotebush (*Larrea tridentata*)	20
Desert Mariposa Lily (*Calochortus kennedyi*)	22
Desert Thorn (*Lycium* spp.)	24
Devil's Claw (*Proboscidea* spp.)	26
Fairy Duster (*Calliandra eriophylla*)	28
Globemallow (*Sphaeralcea ambigua*)	30
Jojoba (*Simmondsia chinensis*)	32
Mesquite (*Prosopis* spp.)	34
Mistletoe (*Phoradendron* spp.)	36
Ocotillo (*Fouquieria splendens*)	38
Paloverde (*Cercidium* spp.)	40
Prickly-Pear (*Platyopuntia* spp.)	42
Reina de la Noche (*Peniocereus greggii*)	44
Saguaro (*Carnegiea gigantea*)	46
Sotol (*Dasylirion wheeleri*)	48
Thorn-Apple (*Datura* spp.)	50
Recommended Reading	52
Acknowledgments	53

Preface

Early in 2023 I set off on a journey to a foreign world, a place that exists only in the ether, with an unfamiliar language and culture. Rumors abounded about ChatGPT, a new and wildly popular AI reputed to be a time-saving tool for writing, while skeptical observers claimed that in the near future AI would replace writers. I decided to open a dialogue with ChatGPT to judge the utility of this revolutionary technology for myself.

My first experimental queries were awkward, uncertain forays into a space built by software engineers, not poets: "Tell me about . . ." and then I would ask about historical events or famous people and receive a brief summary in return. After I asked the AI how to phrase queries, the generated articles became more specific. Additionally, every reply from the AI gave me the opportunity to give it a thumbs-up or thumbs-down rating, as well as to regenerate the query to get a more tailored response. To improve my interactions with ChatGPT further, I learned more about how the AI was trained and how it utilized the vast sea of information in its databanks.

Upon discovering ChatGPT's extensive training on poetry and the individual styles of poets from ancient to modern, I prompted, "Write a poem on a topic of your choosing in your own style." (One of my writing friends would be appalled that I didn't preface my query with "Please.") These are the first and last stanzas of the five-stanza poem produced by the AI in response to this prompt:

> The stars above, a cosmic view,
> A mesmerizing sight to pursue,
> A sight to behold,
> A story untold,
> Of galaxies, stars and nebulae too.
> . . . .
> So let us gaze up at the night sky,
> In awe and wonder, let our hearts fly,
> For the stars above,
> Are a reminder of,
> The infinite beauty of the universe, on high.

The AI's attempt to express emotions in the poem through words such as "mesmerizing," "awe," and "wonder" seemed sophomoric, and the repetitive AABBA rhyming scheme proved persistent through follow-up queries, leading me to wonder whether queries could be phrased in a way that would produce poetry less trite and singsong. What would the AI be capable of writing, lacking the shape of the sounds and the feel of the words in the mouth?

I quickly learned that although ChatGPT can provide descriptions and examples of free verse and prose poems, its responses to the prompt "write a poem . . ." exhibit end rhymes, old-fashioned capitalization and punctuation, and stanzaic construction unless the initial query specifically demands otherwise. (Sometimes, ChatGPT ignores even an explicit limit on the number of requested lines or syllables and goes its own way, like a rebellious teenager.)

In an attempt to guide ChatGPT toward generating more-interesting poetry, I elected to confine the AI to a smaller canvas than the universe. I chose a place with which I am deeply familiar, where two decades of lived experience gave me a rich source of sensations, observations, and incidents to turn into poems: the Sonoran Desert of Arizona. I had already crafted poems on plants and animals of the region before undertaking this project and had written several novels set in the Arizona desert, with that distinctive environment playing a major role in all of them.

A few queries to ChatGPT established that the AI had enough data about the Sonoran Desert ecosystem to generate well-informed responses. But could it write poems that would capture the spirit of the desert? I tested ChatGPT's sense of place using such unique plants as the saguaro, creosotebush, and ocotillo. The results were interesting, yielding poems whose themes reflect many aspects of living in the Sonoran Desert.

Initially I thought I would mix plants and animals together and pair my poems with those of ChatGPT in an all-text book. Then a friend exposed me to some of the amazing images produced by various AIs, from DALL-E (based on ChatGPT-3) to Midjourney and Stable

Diffusion. My initial requests for works styled after Rembrandt, Van Gogh, Monet, and other famous painters produced artistic images of the Sonoran Desert, to which I added variety through prompts specifying different visual media such as botanical illustrations, anime, photorealism, stained glass, and other ways of viewing the world. The AIs usually produced recognizable plants but frequently failed for animals, generating images more appropriate for horror stories than poetry. As a result, this book portrays only the fascinating plants of the Sonoran Desert.

I decided to contrast these AI images with my own photographs to give a realistic, rather than artistic, view of each plant. Thus, each spread, or set of left and right pages, shows my poems and photographs on the left and the AI-generated poems and images on the right.

Overall, ChatGPT's version of life in this desert ecosystem may seem bleak at first glance, focusing on universal themes such as loneliness, strength, and struggle. Yet in the creative journey that the chatbot took in putting concepts into words, elements of the beauty, resilience, and distinctiveness of each plant also emerged.

My own creative journey led me down interesting paths, too. Going through the process of issuing prompts, assessing responses, and providing feedback over and over sharpened my sense of not only what each plant means to me but also what significance it might have within its neighborhood and the larger world. As I developed these poems and images and organized them into a book, the desert that I spent two decades exploring and another two decades writing about became even more fresh and vibrant to me, and I am newly humbled before its startling grandeur.

Whether you are familiar with the Sonoran Desert or this is your first exposure to it, I hope you gain from these pages an enhanced appreciation for this amazing place. Above all, may you enjoy exploring the result of this AI-interaction project as much as I enjoyed creating it. Good reading.

Introduction

> *Poetry is the spontaneous overflow of powerful feelings: it takes its origin from emotion recollected in tranquility.* —William Wordsworth

Spontaneity. Feelings and emotions. Recollections. In Wordsworth's formulation, poetry is the sort of bold venture that emerges from a hike in the desert on an eye-dazzling day in December, a striving to capture the multitude of sensory impressions that surround the hiker. Inspired by such moments, the poet embarks on an introspective quest for words capable of sharing personal experiences with other people.

Lately we have begun to hear that computers are capable of creative writing—essays, fiction, screenplays, even poetry—that is indistinguishable from the works of humans. One might well ask how a computer, lacking emotion and memory, can write a poem. The answer: the computer has been trained to write poetry, therefore it can write poetry. Simple.

Or is it? Is computer-generated poetry really capable of capturing the essence of a place it has never been, a feeling it has never experienced? To find out, I turned to ChatGPT, the best known of these electronic text generators.

OpenAI, the company that developed ChatGPT, describes it as an artificial intelligence (AI) model designed "to generate human-like text and have conversations with humans" with the ultimate goal of making "a more natural and efficient way for humans to interact with machines." In other words, it is a specific type of chatbot, the technology we have become used to seeing on websites and in computer applications such as virtual assistants and customer service chats.

ChatGPT was released for public use in November 2022 and quickly accumulated devotees, with an estimated 100 million active daily users. In spring 2023, ChatGPT-4 became available by subscription, providing advantages including quicker response turnaround. People have begun to use ChatGPT for a variety of tasks, including real-time language translation, summarizing large amounts of text, and content creation.

The AI was trained on a large corpus of text data drawn from sources such as books, articles, and websites, known as a large-language model. In effect, ChatGPT predicts the next word based on the words that came before it, similar to the suggestions offered while writing a text message. The training ended in 2021, so information generated later than that date is generally unavailable.

Fortunately, poetry does not rely on up-to-the-minute facts or trends, and ChatGPT has no shortage of information about poets and poetry. Never plagued by human-like humility, ChatGPT boldly states that there were "millions of poems among the vast amount of text that I was trained on."

ChatGPT undeniably is capable of discussing poems, poets, and poetics at a detailed level. For example, the chatbot can list forms of poetry along with a summary of the dominant characteristics of each, from sonnets and odes to villanelles, ghazals, and sestinas. When asked who was the earliest poet in its dataset, ChatGPT offered the name of Enheduanna (with the caveat that there is no definitive answer), a Sumerian priestess who signed her name to poems on clay tablets circa 2300 BC. I spent countless hours lost in ChatGPT's encyclopedic discussions of the individual style of poets from Shakespeare to Allen Ginsberg. Then I turned to poetics, which the chatbot informed me "seeks to understand the elements that make poetry unique, such as its use of language, form, rhythm, and imagery, and to analyze how these elements work together to create meaning and emotional impact."

As I soon learned, ChatGPT can analyze these elements but has difficulty actually generating poems rich with "meaning and emotional impact." ChatGPT was trained to write poetry by analyzing the structure and patterns of existing poems and using this information to generate new lines of verse following what the chatbot calls "the conventions of poetry, such as using figurative language, employing meter and rhyme, and exploring complex themes and emotions." When challenged about whether its responses might be banal because it is trained to predict the most likely next words, ChatGPT claims that although it lacks "the ability to be creative in the same way that a human writer can be," it can "generate text that is unexpected or surprising" and can "combine and recombine ideas in novel ways."

I decided to take ChatGPT at its word. I began the process of generating poems by asking what syntax to use in the prompts. The chatbot advised, "You can ask me to write a poem by simply providing a prompt or a topic. For example, you could say 'Can you write a poem about love?' or 'Please write a poem about nature.' It's helpful to be as specific as possible with your prompt, as this can help me generate a more focused and relevant poem. You can also provide any additional guidelines or preferences you have for the poem, such as the length, tone, or style. Once I receive your prompt, I will generate a poem and present it to you. You can then provide feedback or ask for revisions if necessary, and I will work to refine the poem until it meets your expectations."

After a few weeks of learning how to word the initial prompts and refine the AI's responses, I began to ask for poems specific to the Sonoran Desert of Arizona. I wrote my own poems first, to make sure my words were not influenced by those of ChatGPT. I had not read poems about the Sonoran Desert for many years, so I could craft my lines without worrying about copying other poets. I utilized a variety of poetic forms and tried to incorporate elements of natural history such as growth habit, flowering time, reproduction, and interactions with other plants and animals, because ChatGPT was likely to have this information in its expansive dataset.

In the AI poems that follow, I kept the editing to a minimum, sometimes trading out one line for another from a different version to avoid repeating the same word for an end-of-line rhyme, occasionally changing a single word that was factually incorrect (where the chatbot described white flowers on a purple-flowering plant, for example, or got the season of blooming wrong), or asking ChatGPT to provide a new line to replace phrases that seemed weak or nonsensical. Thus, in the poem about the fairy duster, I elected not to use this couplet: "Amidst the cactus and the stones, / It stands alone, a vibrancy that drones." There may be ten versions of a poem in my notes, but I chose only the best one to put in the book. Some of the poems actually do "recombine ideas in novel ways"—those are my favorites.

While writing my poems, I searched for appropriate images of desert plants in my collection of photographs, from 35mm color slides and enlargements made several decades ago to digital photos taken for research purposes more recently. I found photographs of about thirty species and selected the plants that were most interesting in terms of natural history or that triggered memories and emotions as I sorted through my past.

Upon finishing my own poem and image for each plant, I asked ChatGPT to write a poem that I hoped would be complementary, whether in form, tone, or focus, often modeled on specific poets or literary traditions such as the Bible or Norse sagas. These poems had to be regenerated, edited, and curated to bring out the "unexpected or surprising" aspects that would make them more interesting for a reader, without employing so much human creativity that they could no longer be considered AI generated.

Finally, there were the AI images to prepare. Each of the image-generating AIs has its own style: weird, eerily realistic, artistic. Most of the AI images used in this book were produced from a text prompt. In the prompts, I tried to capture the essence of each plant rather than expecting it to be portrayed in detail as if in a scientific botanical collection. A few images had to be generated from a photograph, however, because the AI had no idea what these plants looked like.

This was the most time-consuming part of the process, more even than writing my own poems. Generating images requires a lot of computing power and a fast internet connection speed. It means writing a prompt and waiting in a queue behind other people who, like you, want to see the artwork in their imagination made real. When you get to the head of the line, you are shown one or two or four or ten versions of what you asked for, generally realize none of them are appropriate, and have to rewrite the prompt several times and wait some more. Even after all this, quite a few of the AI images have only a nodding acquaintance with reality.

Fortunately, reproducing reality is not the primary goal of poetry. Nor do I expect realism to be the definitive test of ChatGPT and image-generating AIs. I did not embark on this project to criticize AIs or to hold up my own creativity as superior to anything a machine can produce; rather, it was an experiment focused on generating interesting insights about the desert, as well as being an example of collaboration between human and AI.

For ease of comparison between human and computer, each spread, or set of left and right pages, shows my poems and photographs on the left and the AI-generated poems and images on the right. For the AI text and images, I include key words from the prompts.

In theory, every time the AI is given the same prompt, it should produce the same image or the same text. In practice, however, previous queries seemed to influence the elements of a given poem or image, as if weighting some aspect of the AI's algorithm above others. If I asked about free verse, for example, the next poem might have a less strict rhythm and rhyme structure. This unpredictability helped make the project more interesting.

I would never elevate ChatGPT to the same level as a coworker, but figuring out how to frame the prompts to get a desired response felt almost like dealing with someone in the workplace who has an entirely different approach to writing. Thus, although I would not describe the interactions as efficient, they were productive. Overall, I concluded that this latest form of information technology has drawbacks and limitations, but if adopted as widely as the printing press, the typewriter, and the word processor, generative AI has the potential to serve humanity as another tool in our writer's toolbox as we advance into the future.

I hope the examples in this book from ChatGPT and the image-generating AIs inspire other people to go further, expanding the applications for AI in a way that fosters creativity, even among those who have never thought of themselves as poets or authors. For if users can rely on natural-language AIs for everything from brainstorming ideas to editing their own work and improving their writing (as various apps and chatbots promise), more people may see their way to becoming writers. Surely that would be the best possible result of the development of ChatGPT and other generative AIs—not to take jobs away from people and give them to machines but to allow humans to bring more beauty into the world.

Barrel Cactus (*Ferocactus* spp.)

Adorned by a diadem of juicy yellow fruit,
leaning drunkenly aside
from a neighbor grown impertinent,
starred with barbs both hooked and straight
to guard the precious pulp within—
a source of desert water for the bold
but moisture thick and toxic.

Easy to drink in too much
surrounded by a landscape rich in variation,
an explosion of survival strategies,
where spring ephemerals avoid the summer heat
by dying after setting seed,
and leaves drop off when dryness strikes.

After countless generations, stems
took on a barrel's deep-ribbed roundness
to hoard scarce water deep within,
protected by a thorny skin
that bears its chlorophyll behind
a thin coating of waxy hesitation,
miserly presentation by the barrel cactus,
tricking many into thinking it unwelcoming.

But to me it seems an old and precious friend,
a favorite denizen of the Sonoran Desert
to brighten spirit and lighten feet
of this weary traveler gone too long
and recently come home again.

AI on Barrel Cactus

Upon the arid stage of desert's expanse,
there stands an unsung hero, the barrel cactus,
solitary amid the golden sands,
as firm as a yeoman's heart. In form a spiny
scroll of nature's verse, testament to the resilience
of life under the merciless sun,
where the zephyr sings a lullaby of solitude.
It stands, a fortress of green, armored in spikes
as sharp as a falcon's gaze. Each thorn, a pike-man
steadfast in his vigil, arrayed in a phalanx
of fierce defiance against the boundless elements.
Yet within this bulwark, life's sweetest nectar
is stored, a reservoir of hope that slakes
the thirst of creatures desperate under the sun's
relentless rays. Much like the humble king,
who wields not his scepter in vainglory
but in service to his realm, the barrel cactus
stands not in vanity of its form
but in earnest duty. A sentinel of the sand,
a beacon of sustenance, a sage silent
amid the wilderness's whispers.

Prompt (ChatGPT-4): prose poem in the style of William Shakespeare; AI added line breaks to create a free verse poem

AI images (top to bottom): impressionism (DALL-E), watercolor (DALL-E), photorealism (Stable Diffusion)

Brittlebush (*Encelia farinosa*)

Selfish shrub, the yellow-flowered brittlebush
hoards rare rainwater for its roots.
Runoff from its resinous leaves
poisons the soil, killing seeds
of other blooming plants,
for it prefers its own kind
on the land nearby,
companions that follow
the same arcane rules of when to grow,
when to bloom, when to drop the springtime
flush of green and go fallow. A rime
of dust clings to silver foliage
as brittlebush waits for the cool of fall to edge
out summer and call forth waving blooms
above enthusiastic new-leaved stems.
A brittlebush community is what it wants,
untainted by others within its clumps
of sameness, brave in company
but frightened of diversity.

AI on Brittlebush

Brittlebush catches the eye with its bright yellow blooms.
A leafy coating of fine, silver-white hairs
give it a fuzzy appearance. Its leaves, stiff and durable,
turn down to retain moisture in the heat of the day.
As the sun begins to set, the leaves lift up
once more to capture the cooler air
and dew that settle in the evening.
Despite its delicate appearance,
resilient brittlebush survives
in its harsh environment.
Its lack of spines, while a rarity
in the desert, serves as a reminder
that strength can take many forms.

Prompt (ChatGPT): prose poem emphasizing lack of spines; AI added line breaks to create a free verse poem

AI images (clockwise from top): expressionism (Midjourney), watercolor (Midjourney), photorealism (Stable Diffusion), style of O'Keeffe (Midjourney)

Cattail (*Typha domingensis*)

Cattails sink deep roots
where bulrush and carrizo
join floating primrose-willow.
Did you fly far on
weary wings to find this pond?
Nest here in spike-rush
and tussocks of zacatón.

AI on Cattail

Cattails sway in quiet grace.
By the tranquil pond they abide.
A duck glides, leaving no trace.
In mirrored surface, it confides.
Ripples spread in gentle pace.
Nature's secrets, water hides.
Life's serene, peaceful embrace.

Prompt (ChatGPT-4): seven-line poem in choka form about cattails and a duck in a pond, emphasizing tranquility (note that the lines of the poem do not alternate between five and seven syllables as in the traditional Japanese form)

AI images (top to bottom): style of Audubon (Stable Diffusion), style of Van Gogh (Midjourney), style of Van Gogh (Midjourney), quilt (Midjourney)

Century Plant (*Agave* spp.)

spiraling leaves like petals on a rose
set in Fibonacci sequence
from tender center each leaf grows

long and graceful arching form
armed at tip with piercing dagger
each edge lined with clawing thorns

carefully blended artist's palette
in watercolor blue-green hues
embossed with arcs where overlapped

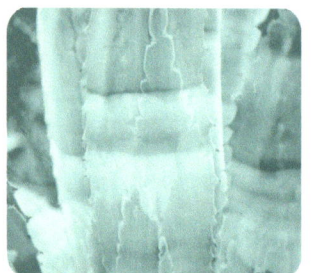

not a sentinel growing alone
but a colonizer preparing the ground
for pups it puts out when full-grown

heart fattened by the desert sun
it sends up one thick flower stalk
and blooms in glorious death hard-won

AI on Century Plant

century plant stands tall and wide
a stoic soul that knows no crime
amid the desert a beacon of pride

its leaves unfold in sunlight gleams
through scorching heat it bides its time
this fabled plant that teems with dreams

it blooms at last in spectacle
towering high to dwell in the sky
in fleeting burst to life farewell

as petals fall the cycle turns
but in this finale a message it sends
in arid land new life returns

century plant in the desert sun's glow
from your journey a truth descends
life persists amid ebb and flow

Prompt (ChatGPT-4): five-stanza poem with three lines in each stanza using the rhyme scheme ABA

AI images: (top) photorealism, (all others) botanical illustration (all from Midjourney)

Cholla (*Cylindropuntia* spp.)

Chainfruit, teddy-bear,
staghorn, pencil cholla—
pronounced CHOY-a—
all examples of *Cylindropuntia*,
a crazy sticklike cactus
that latches on with sharp barbed spines.
These broken stems get carried off
to fresh locations,
there to root and grow anew.
Carry a fine-toothed comb
if you go walking near a cholla thicket,
to flick the stem away without inflicting
damage on your fingers.
When too old to live another day,
the fearsome spines and silky flesh
shrink and fall to leave a skeleton
like crocheted wood, the only sign
of what once came from far away
and made this space its own.

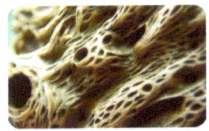

AI on Cholla

Cholla cacti, strange and beautiful,
Stand as desert spectacles.
Growing in clusters, their spiny, jointed stems
Erupt in brilliant yellow or red blooms.
Some species present smooth, round bodies,
While others are rough, angular,
Their spines long, curved like fallen needles.

Behold the teddy bear cholla,
Whimsical in its fluffy guise,
Seemingly hugging the air with spindly arms.
But beware its innocent charm,
For beneath soft appearances, it defends,
A painful sting concealed within eager spines.

The chain-fruit cholla, heavy and low,
Droops under the weight of bountiful fruit.
An abundance it offers to the desert,
Attracting rabbits, squirrels,
Insect pollinators and birds,
A hub of life in the barren expanse.

AI images (top to bottom): bronze, cartoon, black-and-white photo, photorealism (all from Midjourney)

The jumping cholla, a mischievous dweller,
Detaches and leaps, hooks onto passersby.
Despite its tricky reputation, it too has a place,
Offering a home, food for desert creatures,
An unlikely refuge in the sand and stone.

These are but a few faces of the cholla,
Each unique in character, yet united in purpose,
They all play their part in the desert's dance,
A cycle of life and death,
Unfolding under the harsh, unforgiving sun.

Prompt (ChatGPT-3): prose poem about multiple species of cholla; ChatGPT-4 added line breaks to create a free verse poem

Common Reed (*Phragmites communis*)

A giant reed once lined the banks, bamboolike leafy *Phragmites*,
Now vanished, hidden in the sand.
No longer found in thickets deep, this common native species,
Which formerly did drought and flood withstand.

Now vanished, hidden in the sand,
Are those who once cut down the reeds
Which formerly did drought and flood withstand—
The hollow stems sufficed for games and many needs.

Are those who once cut down the reeds
A mystery, leaving only fragmentary hints of what they made?
The hollow stems sufficed for games and many needs
When split and woven into mats and panels casting shade.

A mystery, leaving only fragmentary hints of what they made
In dry caves in the desert—for little lasts of reedy grass
When split and woven into mats and panels casting shade,
Or the guessing game the people played, each other to surpass.

In dry caves in the desert—though little lasts of reedy grass—
Remain cigarettes of cane, and flutes, and tubes used for
The guessing game the people played, each other to surpass,
The Hohokam, "those who are gone," playing games no more.

No longer found in thickets deep, this common native species,
The giant reed that lined the banks, bamboolike leafy *Phragmites*.

AI on Common Reed

In desert's heart where rivers thread,
Grows the common reed, humble, unpretentious.
Against golden sand, a ribbon of green spread,
Standing tall, their whispers hushed, momentous.

Grows the common reed, humble, unpretentious,
Under the harsh glare of the sun.
Standing tall, their whispers hushed, momentous,
They sway and dance, their journey begun.

Under the harsh glare of the sun,
Azure dome pierced by their green spires,
They sway and dance, their journey begun,
In the barren land, a sight to admire.

Azure dome pierced by their green spires
Beside the river, they have found their home.
In the barren land, a sight to admire
Where the desert winds softly comb.

Beside the river, they have found their home.
In the desert's quiet narrative,
Where the desert winds softly comb,
The common reed is illustrative.

Against golden sand, a ribbon of green spread,
In desert's heart where rivers thread.

Prompt (ChatGPT-4): poem about common reed growing beside rivers in the desert; AI rewrote the poem in the form of a pantoum

AI images (top to bottom): Mexican mural style, botanical illustration, Mexican mural style (all from Midjourney)

Creosotebush (*Larrea tridentata*)

Bitter scent of rain
snagged in resinous leaves of green
lingers as a distant memory,
while faded wintry twigs clutch tight
to flower tufts of creamy white—
at every heart a seed,
a single fleck of brown
that someday drifts upon a breeze
far from its home of twisted branches.
For now the sprawling bush languishes
in short cold days
and wishes for the intense heat
and pounding storms of summer
to coax forth sun-yellow flowers.

AI on Creosotebush

Larrea tridentata stands alone and strong,
its leaves a shield against harsh winter winds,
offering shelter to those who seek
respite from the desert's biting chill.
Seeds scattered in promise wait
on the desert floor through the heat of summer,
as the tough shrub remains steadfast, undeterred
by the blazing sun, anchoring its roots deep
in the earth. Unyielding, the creosotebush persists,
a beacon of resilience in a land of extremes,
a survivor of all, standing watch over the desert
like a solitary sentinel.

Prompt (ChatGPT-4): free verse in the style of Emily Dickinson; prose poem based on the free verse; AI added line breaks to the resulting prose poem

AI images (top to bottom): botanical illustration, photo, style of Klimt, style of Rembrandt (all from Stable Diffusion)

Desert Mariposa Lily (*Calochortus kennedyi*)

folded fragility of fiery hue
spindly stem sliding forth
leaves long in languid serenity
exquisite elusive ephemeral life
hasty hours on hillside evanescent

AI on Desert Mariposa Lily

majestic mystifying marvelous flowers,
fabulously flourishing, fantastically golden,
glowing gently in grandeur peaceful,
a pleasing panorama of picturesque dancing
in dazzling desert daring, a thriving,
tenacious tangerine tapestry, so merry

Prompt (ChatGPT-4): poem with five words on each line, and all the words in a given line must start with the same letter; regenerated four times to create many options (editing: words shifted and articles and prepositions added for sense)

AI images (top to bottom): Mexican mural, anime (both from Midjourney)

Desert Thorn (*Lycium* spp.)

gray-green silver and subtle pastel purple
fill out the scanty palette of hues
worn by a common brushy shrub
after soaking rains of winter

leaves sneak skyward first thirsty
for the gentle short-day sun
twisting off-true every which way
to follow light beyond the shadows

tucked under flat-fleshed leaves
peering forth in floral humility
half-hidden blooms fill the joints
all along flexible thin branches

space enough between for dancing
butterflies whose wings slip in
and tongues unfurl to sip
upon sweet nectar

once flowers fade the bush
strengthens its story as heavy red fruit
grows thick upon the twigs
attracting eager birds who spread the seeds

but finally the desert thorn
sinks back into obscurity
to wait for chilly rains
once more in quiet guarded reverie

AI on Desert Thorn

desert thorn blooms with a quiet grace,
its small flowers dotting the landscape
in subtle shades of pink and purple

leaves are a silvery-green,
shimmering in the desert sun
as thorny branches twist and curl

desert thorn fruit, small and red,
is packed with nutrients and sweetness
coveted by birds and humans alike

this resilient shrub thrives in the harshest conditions,
withstanding the heat and drought of the desert
with stoic determination

Lycium embodies the essence of the desert,
a survivor of a harsh and unforgiving landscape,
yet capable of providing sustenance and beauty

Prompt (ChatGPT-4): free verse poem in five three-line stanzas; prose poem based on the free verse; AI added line breaks to the resulting prose poem (editing: lines from different versions combined to avoid rhymes)

AI images (top to bottom): impressionism, art deco, pen and ink, black-and-white photo (all from Midjourney)

Devil's Claw (*Proboscidea* spp.)

Famed not for flowers but the strange pods
that bear its seeds—pendulous,
pulpy, and crooked. When dry, the ripe
black claws split in two, forming hooks
that catch and cling, dragged off to spread
potential life to sites nearby.
Alive, an unassuming plant,
yet its cast-off pieces, dropped and forgotten,
take on a glorious reason for existence
when emptied of the burden of biological purpose.
The claws become materials for beautiful baskets
once soaked, softened, and stripped,
yin-yang woven in dark designs upon a lighter
beargrass ground. Essential component
of indigenous objects of functional art,
the claws trade round the world in seedless,
sterile form, valued anew, traveling farther
than the mother plant will ever know.

AI on Devil's Claw

Amid desert sands,
devil's claw stands proudly
piercing earth below.

Fruits burst forth with promise,
a gift of wild spiraled claws—
nature's artistry.

In the dry desert,
its grasping seeds scatter wide—
nature's generosity.

Harvested with care,
its roots hold healing within—
nature's medicine.

Devil's claw, a sign
of endurance in the wild—
nature's treasure.

Prompt (ChatGPT-4): five-stanza poem about devil's claw using haiku for each stanza (editing: lines from different versions combined to follow haiku syllable count as closely as possible)

AI images (top to bottom): tempera, pen and ink, botanical illustration of pod in black and white (all from Midjourney)

Fairy Duster (*Calliandra eriophylla*)

Filled with blooms in winter,
spring, and sometimes summer,
when watered well by timely rains,
the fairy duster loyally retains
its leaves when other plants lie bare.
Its flowers extrude dainty tufts,
powder-puffs of rose-pink fluff—
the visual display a show to draw in
passing butterflies, pink-tipped stamens
bringing insects by for pollination,
a generous libation on a dry hillside.
The fairy duster's seeds, flung wide,
will fall on rocky ground designed
for more to grow nearby. Spreading
from mother plant in an evolutionary dance,
the seedlings slowly colonize the bare expanse,
creating a blaze of bright-hued blossoming,
until the showy stamens droop in slow decline,
slipping off and leaving dull seedpods behind.
What lesson do we learn from this? That beauty
must inevitably fade? Or do we drop our gloomy
fears and look for evidence
that even in the arid desert,
life will find a way?

AI on Fairy Duster

The fairy duster blooms,
a secret garden in plain view,
a beacon of beauty, a sign of life
in the midst of strife, a fairy's wand,
nature's grand stand in a barren land.
In the heat of day it stands alone
among the cactus and the stones,
a vibrant burst of red and pink,
a fairy dance on desert's brink,
delicate beauty, in the dust it thrives,
a ray of sunshine in the desert's shade,
a reminder of life in a land of decay.

Prompt (ChatGPT-3): free verse in the style of Billy Collins; free verse in the style of Emily Dickinson; (ChatGPT-4) poem about fairy duster with no end rhyme (editing: lines from AI-generated poem versions combined)

AI images (top to bottom): oil painting, pointillism, photorealistic landscape (all from Stable Diffusion)

Globemallow (*Sphaeralcea ambigua*)

Globemallow, with its gray-blue faded leaves,
Lobed threefold and bearing hairs
Of velvety temptation, casts away caution and
Blooms as it pleases,
Each plant choosing its time, as on
Many stems—dozens, a hundred—
Apricot flowers, orange, or red,
Lick fiercely up the stem
Like fiery embers,
Offering a challenge to the sun—
We shine here!

AI on Globemallow

Glistening in the sun,
Luminous and lively,
Overwhelming with its
Beauty and grace.
Every petal unique, like a fingerprint,
Making each flower a piece of art,
All of them together creating a sea of pink.
Low and slow it sways, with
Lush petals soft as silk.
Of all the flowers, this one shines the brightest,
Waving in the breeze.

Prompt (ChatGPT): 11-line acrostic poem for the word "GLOBEMALLOW" (editing: lines from three AI-generated poems combined)

AI images (top to bottom): style of Monet, style of Mondragon (both from Stable Diffusion)

Jojoba (*Simmondsia chinensis*)

nigh higher slopes
along mountain trails
grow low, and slowly,
thigh-high shrubs
with fingerlike leaves
of off-true bluish hue
leaning greeny silver—
tough stuff from rough
rocky soil, toiling to drain
thirsting terrain nearby
of pore-stored water
to feed seeds heavy
and hard to pry open
to reach the prized oil inside

AI on Jojoba

In the heart of the desert
where the sun bears down
with relentless intensity,
the jojoba bush stands,
a monument to life's tenacity.

Its leaves, a muted gray-green,
press stiff against the wind,
whispering secrets of survival
in an arid expanse where existence
often hangs by a thread.

Its roots, buried deep
within the parched earth,
draw sustenance from hidden
springs and reservoirs below.

Jojoba's very presence tells a tale
of adaptation, of an indomitable spirit
that refuses to be extinguished,
even in the harshest of landscapes.

Prompt (ChatGPT-4): two-paragraph prose poem; AI added line breaks to change prose poem to free verse with four stanzas

Note: jojoba is pronounced ho-HO-ba

AI images (top to bottom): style of Matisse, cartoon, cubism (all from Midjourney)

Mesquite (*Prosopis* spp.)

I.
Not all trees need to be useful—
beauty speaks in human tongues,
a universal primal language
uttered first by nameless ancients
who viewed sunsets through thin branches,
rested there, and sighed in wonder.

Deep-rooted mesquite in the desert
taps a soft and peaceful well
within the bones of weary travelers.
For the mesquite provides shelter,
a place to rest and watch the sun
set behind the toothy mountains,
daunting destinations to be
faced and overcome
on the next day's journey.

II.
Unlikely haven is the mesquite,
so rough-barked and filled with sap,
pressing crooked, thorny twigs
toward the sky, its leaves crocheting
formless patterns in the air.
In this pleasant sanctuary
from the blazing desert sun
I once stole many moments,
making drowsy memories
that carried me through endless winters
in the cold and snowy North.

Now I think back to the dreamtime
underneath the twisty branches
and wish I could regain the days
I journeyed far away.

AI on Mesquite

A mesquite tree stands solitary
in the heart of the desert.
Its silhouette, twisted and gnarled,
outlines a story of resilience
against the vast, sun-bleached canvas
of sand and sky.

Humble yet tenacious beacon of life,
it has tapped into the arid soil's reservoirs,
its roots like veins threading
through the desert's hard heart.
The whisper of greenery it offers becomes
a hymn to life in a realm dominated
by relentless sun and heat.

Look at its branches, they reach out
like skeletal arms, each one etching
a narrative of survival against
capricious desert elements—
scorching sun, biting wind, chilling frost.
These arms offer a coveted refuge,
a spot of shade under sparse foliage,
a sanctuary in the desert's vast cathedral.

Here, beneath the mesquite, life stirs,
unseen, unheard, but palpably present
in the hushed rustle of leaves
and the shadowed coolness
against the searing heat.

Prompt (ChatGPT-4): three-paragraph prose poem; AI added line breaks to change prose poem to free verse with four stanzas

AI images (top to bottom): minimalism, photorealism, impressionism, fresco (all from Midjourney)

Mistletoe (*Phoradendron* spp.)

Not the dainty sprig for kissing
under but a wild growth—
"before" hair in shampoo ads,
sticking out in all directions,
abandoning any sense of shame,
like bristling porcupine or sea urchin
in shades of green.

Parasite upon the tree, yet only drawing
what it needs. Both survive,
host and uninvited guest,
unless the overgrowth becomes
too greedy. Then both die.

AI on Mistletoe

In the quiet stillness of the desert,
mistletoe hangs like a mystical charm,
a symbol of resilience in a land of extremes.
It's a curious sight to behold in the branches
of its host, drawing forth water and nutrients
yet photosynthesizing on its own,
independent. Its presence in the desert
only adds to its mystique and allure.
Its berries nourish birds and other desert wildlife.
Its presence breaks up the monotony
of the desert's winter landscape,
adding a touch of greenery and color.
Its unique ability to thrive serves as a reminder
that life can flourish in the most unlikely places,
offering a sense of hope and interconnectedness,
binding all living things in an endless cycle
of life and death.

Prompt (ChatGPT): prose poem about desert mistletoe in a mesquite tree; ChatGPT-4 added line breaks to change prose poem to free verse

AI images (top to bottom): botanical illustration, stylized, impressionism (all from Midjourney)

Ocotillo (*Fouquieria splendens*)

Ocotillo, coachwhip, firethorn,
melok, candlewood, flaming sword,
slimwood, vinecactus, Jacob's staff,
many names of what it's not—
not a cactus, whip, or candle,
not a sword or thorn,
neither vine nor wooden,
and a painful staff to hold.

To grow it at your will,
hack off a stem, insert it in the ground
to root and grow where planted.
It makes a living fence,
readily accepting a new place as its home,
exhibiting an urge to thrive
that cannot be resisted.

Its needs are simple—
sunlight, water, dirt, and pollination.
It has no need to be admired
but makes fantastical presentation
in silhouette against a streaky dawn.
In dry spells, leaves are gone,
growing back with ample rain,
green and brown in alternation.

Its blooming time coincides
with hummingbird migration
northward in the spring,
red-orange tubes providing nectar
to fuel the tiny birds a-wing.
Later, seeds feed scrabbling desert creatures.
Well suited for the dryland life,
this spiky plant accommodates its neighbors.

AI on Ocotillo

In the scorching heat of the desert,
the ocotillo stands tall, a beacon of hope and life.
Its spindly branches stretch toward the sky,
reaching for the sun. A symbol
of resilience in an unforgiving landscape,
ocotillo's vibrant red flowers bloom in bursts,
painting the desert in vibrant hues,
attracting a host of buzzing bees
and fluttering hummingbirds
as its roots reach deep into the ground.
Despite its tough exterior, the ocotillo's balance
of strength and fragility reminds us
of the importance of adaptation in the face
of adversity, and the power of nature
to persist and thrive
even in the harshest of conditions.

Prompt (ChatGPT-4): prose poem about Fouquieria splendens *as part of the desert ecosystem; AI added line breaks to change prose poem to free verse*

Note: ocotillo is pronounced oh-coh-TEE-oh

AI images (top to bottom): painting, ink (both from Midjourney)

Paloverde (*Cercidium* spp.)

"Green stick," its name proclaims,
green from ground to thorny tip—

even leafless, laid bare for the daily
chlorophyll conversion of the sun's hard rays
to feed deep roots,

even during times of drought
when dusty brush around the trunk
has shriveled into nothingness,

even in the flush of springtime bloom, when cloaked
by yellow clouds of flowers, still the paloverde's canopy
offers gentle peeks of green,

even rising out of steep-sloped rocks
or gravel on broad desert pavement flats
or waiting for water to flow along washes,

paloverde paints a single splash of color
in a monochrome monotony.

AI on Paloverde

Paloverde, desert's green beacon,
reaching skyward, roots deep driven.

Spring adorns you in yellow blossoms,
nature's fireworks, ephemeral display,
a silent celebration of survival.

Bright against a stark, arid canvas,
bouncing back the sun's fierce glare,
life thriving on borrowed chances.

Shelter offered to desert wanderers,
in your arms, a haven found,
against the silent, scorching summers.

Paloverde, resilient and profound,
in you, the desert's heart bursts forth,
life's tenacity in each leaf, each twig.

A resting place for desert creatures,
brief respite from desolation.

Prompt (ChatGPT-4): 15-line poem in free verse using 3-line stanzas (note that the poem has 16 lines, with two 2-line stanzas)

AI images (clockwise from top): oil painting, wire sculpture, photorealism, stained glass (all from Stable Diffusion)

Prickly-Pear (*Platyopuntia* spp.)

Surreptitious itchy spines,
the kind that hide inside
white fuzzy tufts
spaced evenly on skin
a rosy sunset hue.
So tempting to approach
and with a testing finger
broach the question
whether soft and smooth
as satin is the glossy
cactus pad beneath
its fluffy velvet-seeming coat.

AI on Prickly-Pear

Prickly-pear,
moist, succulent,
surviving the desert.
Sharp spines, vibrant flowers, sweet fruit,
adapted.

Prickly-pear, oh how you thrive,
tough and strong, thick pads.
After bloom, fruits grow.
Beneath the scorching sunshine,
you persist, so proud.

Nourish,
sustaining life,
symbol of resilience,
enduring beauty in harsh land,
prickly-pear.

Prompt (ChatGPT-4): two-stanza cinquain with a third stanza in choka form

AI images (top to bottom): style of Picasso, simplified version of Picasso image above (both from Midjourney)

Reina de la Noche (*Peniocereus greggii*)

Sere thorny stick transforms one summer's night each year,
with showy moonglow flowers beaming to the sky,
richly scented, tempting pollinators near.
Sere thorny stick transforms one summer's night each year.
Come day, white petals close and disappear
as if ashamed of their display and turning shy.
Sere thorny stick transforms one summer's night each year,
with showy moonglow flowers beaming to the sky.

Awkward is this cactus, in appearance graceless,
unlike its noble name, reina de la noche,
"queen of the night"—a snap judgment quite useless.
Awkward is this cactus, in appearance graceless,
blameless it grows as the wind blows, twisted and shapeless,
unsightly tangle but for a brief blooming display.
Awkward is this cactus, in appearance graceless,
unlike its noble name, reina de la noche.

Throughout the long hours of dark it rules in beauty,
unchallenged by any other bloom, spreading perfume
through the air, queen of the summer night absolutely.
Throughout the long hours of dark it rules in beauty,
drawing hawkmoths and bats to pollination duty,
then flowers fade and months of dethroned obscurity resume.
Throughout the long hours of dark it rules in beauty,
unchallenged by any other bloom, spreading perfume.

AI on Reina de la Noche

Reina de la noche blooms
Under the moon's embrace.
Cactus flowers, secrets loom.
Reina de la noche blooms.
Nightly beauty, sweet perfume
Draws the heart into her space.
Reina de la noche blooms
Under the moon's embrace.

In the desert's silent room,
Stars reflect her grace
Where her petals softly bloom.
In the desert's silent room
Her allure dispels the gloom,
A queen in a barren place.
In the desert's silent room,
Stars reflect her grace.

Prompt (ChatGPT-4): pantoum form (note that the eight-line stanzas generated by the AI do not fit the requested form)

Note: reina de la noche (pronounced RAY-na de la NO-chay) is Spanish for "queen of the night"

AI images (top to bottom): photorealistic stems, minimalism, photorealistic flower, cartoon (all from Midjourney)

Saguaro (*Carnegiea gigantea*)

Protected by a paloverde's overarching shield of green
or mesquite's thorny thick-barked branches,
a fingerling saguaro built its strength amid the gravel,
adding girth and height throughout the seasons,
until it died and left a skeleton, a cylinder
of wooden ribs stuck together out of habit
after death's dry misery
sucked all moisture from the fleshy folds.
Once it stood tall sentinel, majestic guard
for flaming sunset sky, witness to the flower-petal
pink and purple streaks of rising sun.
Scars from ancient damage slowly hardened into cavities
where owls laid eggs and raised their families,
feathered babies taking wing without a care
for sinister arrays of thorns that ringed the opening.
Far above, a crown of creamy flowers capped
the central trunk and many arms,
celebrating steamy days of rising summer,
offering sweet nectar to fat-bodied bats and doves,
whose thirsty revels later led to lush red fruit
split open to reveal a trove of small black seeds,
which fell upon the ground, where a lucky few
began the patient cycle of saguaro's slow renewal.

AI on Saguaro

Saguaro cactus stands, a sacred being in the desert,
its arms outstretched like a prayer to the sky.
From a small seed it begins its journey,
growing slowly tall and strong in the heat of the sun.
Each added arm is a testament to the passing of time,
each pleated fold in its towering frame
like the lines etched into the face of an elder.
Saguaro blooms in early summer, its white flowers
celebrating life in a land of death, its red fruits
a reminder of the power of regeneration.
Saguaro provides food and shelter for creatures
from birds and bees to rodents and reptiles.
Its spines offer protection from the harsh elements
and predators, a barrier between life and death
in a world of extremes. In the shadow of the saguaro,
one can feel the ancient heartbeat of the desert,
the persevering rhythm of life and death
playing out in an endless cycle of renewal.
As seasons change and many years pass by,
the cactus withers and falls to the earth,
but its spirit lives on in new growth nearby
and in the stories told of the saguaro's life.

Prompt (ChatGPT-4): free verse poem in the style of Joy Harjo describing the life cycle of saguaro cactus; poem (with end rhymes) copied into new prompt to generate a prose poem in the style of Joy Harjo; AI added line breaks to the resulting prose poem to create a free verse poem

Note: saguaro is pronounced sa-WAH-row

AI images (top to bottom): style of Monet, impressionist flower, cartoon fruit, style of Van Gogh (all from Stable Diffusion)

Sotol (*Dasylirion wheeleri*)

Belying tooth-edged leaves, deceptive grasslike ball in form—
to warn unwary hikers, posters pinned to walls inform.

A fountain of green grassy needles vertical at first,
blades sag and sink with age to casual sprawling form.

Inviting careless hands to brush across a gray-green puff
till altered by a flower spike to silhouette tall in form.

Eager bees and hummingbirds sip from blossoms, thirsty
winged bodies crowding close, companions small in form.

Also known as desert spoon for inward curve where leaf
meets trunk, a skirt of dead leaves cling to hide the lolling form.

Never giving up the urge to hold to where they emerged,
persisting like the plant for years, messy and informal.

This marvel of a desert shrub has little need for water
but soaks up summer sun to grow arboreal in form.

It has its human uses too—an alcoholic beverage,
thatching, mats, and baskets of enthralling form.

Not a low-desert resident, preferring broader
grasslands where its thin leaves seem more natural in form.

No poem can capture its mysteries, for words transform—
a mere beginning can this be, a brief attempt to inform.

AI on Sotol

In the desert, where the sotol holds sway, each day,
Under the sun's harsh rule, leaves bend, but do not break, each day.

Toothed leaves, like swords, guard their heart, fierce in their array,
Against the wind, they stand tall, a resilience they don't shake, each day.

The arid earth, their cradle, their home, their ballet,
In its silence, their roots deeper make, each day.

Their blooms reach for the sky, a lofty display,
In this barren expanse, they partake, each day.

In their essence, a poet finds a pathway,
Scribing verses in the sand, for their sake, each day.

Prompt (ChatGPT-4): ghazal using a specified pattern of rhyme and repetition described by ChatGPT in a separate query

Note: sotol is pronounced SOH-tohl

AI images (top to bottom): art deco, stained glass (both from Midjourney)

Thorn-Apple (*Datura* spp.)

bold bloom
strong sweet fragrance
delirious night view
blossoms squeeze tight in dawn's sunlight
    and wait

days pass
    after flower
spiny globe filled with seeds
potent procreative effort
    engaged

shamans
    sought altered state
        through seeds and flower dew
risky, this hallucinogen's
    poison

belied
    by fragile show
        of dainty blossoms fresh
nightshade cousin of tomato—
    toxic

AI on Thorn-Apple

datura
blooms in twilight
whispers of mystery
veiled in the cloak of the night—
    dream's seed

moon's charm
scented whispers
guiding the moth's soft flight
    in the silent dance of the night—
        lured in

temptress
    with white petals
        guarding her heart of gold
under stars she unfolds her soul—
    night's bloom

Prompt (ChatGPT-4): didactic cinquain using specified number of syllables (2, 4, 6, 8, 2) in each line (note that syllable count is occasionally incorrect)

AI images (top to bottom): watercolor bud, stylized seedpod, style of O'Keeffe, cartoon (all from Midjourney)

Recommended Reading

- *At the Desert's Green Edge: An Ethnobotany of the Gila River Pima*, by Amadeo Rea, sumi-e illustrations by Takashi Ijichi (University of Arizona Press, 1997)
- *Desert Wildflowers*, text by Desert Botanical Garden staff, photography by Arizona Highways contributors (Arizona Highways Book Division, 1988)
- *A Field Guide to the Plants of Arizona*, by Anne Orth Epple, photography by Lewis E. Epple (Falcon Publishing, 1995)
- *Flowers of the Southwest Deserts*, by Natt N. Dodge, illustrations by Jeanne R. Janish (Southwest Parks and Monuments Association, 1976)
- *Gathering the Desert*, by Gary Paul Nabhan, illustrations by Paul Mirocha (University of Arizona Press, 1985)
- *Going to Seed: Finding, Identifying, and Preparing Edible Plants of the Southwest*, by Kahanah Farnsworth (Ancient City Press, 1999)
- *Healing with Plants in the American and Mexican West*, by Margarita Artschwager Kay (University of Arizona Press, 1996)
- *Landscaping for Desert Wildlife*, by Carolyn Engel-Wilson, photography by George Andrejko and Carolyn Engel-Wilson (Arizona Game and Fish Department, 1992)
- *A Natural History of the Sonoran Desert*, edited by Stephen J. Phillips and Patricia Wentworth Comus (Arizona-Sonora Desert Museum Press, 2000)
- *100 Desert Wildflowers of the Southwest*, by Janice Emily Bowers (Southwest Parks and Monuments Association, 1989)

Acknowledgments

I am grateful to the many poets who have inspired me over the years, especially those who have participated along with me at conferences and workshops such as the Tennessee Mountain Writers' poetry sessions led by wonderful instructors including Stellasue Lee, Lisa Coffman, and Jeff Hardin.

Critiques by fellow members of the monthly Knoxville–Oak Ridge Poetry Critique Group have improved my poetry immeasurably. Many thanks to all of you for reading my poems, supporting me with kind words, and encouraging me to be productive.

Hearing magnificent local poets such as Marilyn Kallet, Linda Parsons, and Rhea Carmon perform their own works in person has added a vivid musical dimension to an art form I previously thought of as textual. I appreciate those poets' willingness to share such transcendent moments more than they will ever know.

I developed confidence in putting words together while enrolled in the University of Wisconsin's Creative Writing program under the direction of Kelly Cherry: thank you for giving me a solid foundation. I must express deep gratitude to the Knoxville Writer's Guild's Advanced Fiction Writers critique group for making me a better writer—in particular to Pamela Schoenewaldt, who read my work outside the group and gave me suggestions for improving this manuscript.

www.ingramcontent.com/pod-product-compliance
Lightning Source LLC
LaVergne TN
LVHW070437080526
838202LV00038B/2840